TENTS

What Makes Penguins Special?

Penguins are flightless birds that mostly live in the cooler parts of the southern oceans. There are no other birds quite like them. On land, they waddle along upright like small, clumsy people, but in the water, they are transformed into graceful, speeding torpedoes. Penguins spend up to three quarters of their lives in the water, only coming to land or sea ice in order to breed. Most of them nest in vast colonies of as many as a million individuals. They have complex courtship displays and many aspects of their lives and behavior are still a mystery, especially the time they spend at sea. Even the origin of the name penguin is not clear. Penguigo means "fat" in Spanish; Spanish sailors were probably first to use the word for the fat auks and divers of the Northern Hemisphere, which look like penguins.

▲ **FLYING UNDERWATER**
Most other diving birds push themselves through the water using their feet, but penguins use their wings, called flippers. When it swims fast, a penguin draws its head into its shoulders and presses its feet close to the body.

BUILT TO SWIM ▶
With their compact, streamlined bodies, short, stiff wings, and rudderlike feet and tail, penguins are superbly suited for swimming. Their legs are far back on their bodies, so they do not stick out and interrupt the streamlined shape. The feet are strong and webbed, each with three hooked toes for gripping slippery rocks and ice. Short, densely packed feathers form a waterproof coat over the whole body.

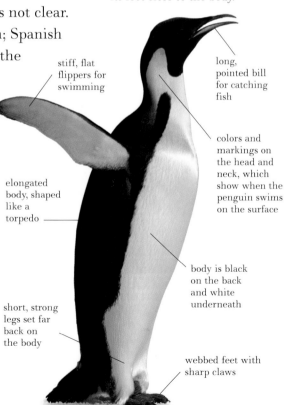

stiff, flat flippers for swimming

long, pointed bill for catching fish

colors and markings on the head and neck, which show when the penguin swims on the surface

elongated body, shaped like a torpedo

body is black on the back and white underneath

short, strong legs set far back on the body

webbed feet with sharp claws

Na t l e

Penguins

Barbara Taylor
Consultant: Michael Chinery

southwater

C O N

This edition is published by Southwater

Southwater is an imprint of
Anness Publishing Ltd
Hermes House, 88–89 Blackfriars Road
London SE1 8HA
tel. 020 7401 2077; fax 020 7633 9499
www.southwaterbooks.com; info@anness.com

© Anness Publishing Ltd 2003, 2005

UK agent: The Manning Partnership Ltd
6 The Old Dairy, Melcombe Road
Bath BA2 3LR
tel. 01225 478444; fax 01225 478440
sales@manning-partnership.co.uk

UK distributor: Grantham Book Services Ltd
Isaac Newton Way, Alma Park Industrial Estate
Grantham, Lincs NG31 9SD
tel. 01476 541080 fax 01476 541061
orders@gbs.tbs-ltd.co.uk

North American agent/distributor:
National Book Network, 4501 Forbes Boulevard
Suite 200, Lanham, MD 20706
tel. 301 459 3366; fax 301 429 5746
www.nbnbooks.com

Australian agent/distributor:
Pan Macmillan Australia
Level 18 St Martins Tower, 31 Market St
Sydney, NSW 2000;
tel. 1300 135 113; fax 1300 135 103
customer.service@macmillan.com.au

New Zealand agent/distributor:
David Bateman Ltd, 30 Tarndale Grove,
Off Bush Road, Albany, Auckland
tel. (09) 415 7664; fax (09) 415 8892

Publisher: Joanna Lorenz
Managing Editor: Linda Fraser
Editor: Sarah Uttridge
Editorial Reader: Lindsay Zamponi
Production Controller: Darren Price
Designer: Linda Penny
Illustrators: A Durante (Milan Illustrations
    Agency)
Picture Researcher: Su Alexander

Previously published as *Nature Watch: Penguins*

10 9 8 7 6 5 4 3 2 1

▼ CHAT SHOW

When penguins come to land to breed, they communicate with a variety of calls and displays. These Gentoo penguins are performing an "ecstatic display," during which they stretch up and call loudly. All penguins, except the Emperor and the Little penguin, perform this display. It helps penguins to reinforce their claim to a nest site, to attract mates, and to deter rivals.

▲ LITTLE LAND LUBBERS

Even though penguins are most at home in the water, they depend on land for breeding, raising their young, and molting. Most penguins breed once a year, laying one or two eggs in the spring and rearing chicks during the summer. After the chicks have grown their feathers, most penguin parents molt their own feathers.

▼ NORTHERN LOOK-ALIKES

Birds in the auk family, such as puffins, guillemots, and this little auk, all look a bit like penguins because they have a similar lifestyle. Both auks and penguins have small wings which they use to swim underwater as they chase prey. The difference is that auks can also use their wings for flying. Auks and penguins never meet, because auks only live north of the equator.

FLIGHTLESS GIANT ▼

Penguins are not the only birds that cannot fly. Other flightless birds include the ostrich, the kiwi, and the flightless cormorant. Their ancestors used to be able to fly, millions of years ago, but lost the power to fly, either because they had few enemies or became too heavy.

Brush-tails and Crests

There are 17 species, or kinds, of penguin, gathered into six groups called genera. On these two pages, you can find out about two of these genera: the Brush-tailed penguins and the Crested penguins. The Brush-tailed penguins include the Adélie, Gentoo, and Chinstrap species, which all have long tail feathers that seem to sweep the ground behind them like a brush. The Crested penguins include the Rockhopper, Macaroni, Royal, Fjordland-crested, Erect-crested, and Snares Island species, which all have colored plumes of feathers above their eyes, like long, feathery eyebrows.

▲ TOUGH CUSTOMERS
Adélie penguins are around 28 inches long and weigh 9 lbs. They have a white ring around their eye. Adélies are one of the toughest penguins, breeding on the coast of the frozen Antarctic continent and nearby islands. The breeding population of Adélies is around 2.5 million pairs. They are good divers, and feed on fish and krill.

▼ GENTLE GENTOO
Gentoos have large, white marks on top of the head. They are slightly larger than Adélies and Chinstraps—they stand 35 inches tall and weigh 13 lbs. Timid and unaggressive, Gentoos prefer to enter the sea from a beach rather than jump from a ledge. They fish deeper than many other species, diving down to over 300 feet. About 314,000 pairs breed on the Antarctic peninsula and subantarctic islands.

▲ NOISY NEIGHBORS
Chinstraps are among the most common penguins. Some 7.5 million pairs breed on the Antarctic peninsula and subantarctic islands in the south Atlantic, such as South Shetland, and South Georgia. On the Antarctic peninsula, they may breed alongside Adélies. Chinstraps are slightly smaller and more aggressive than Adélies, and have an ear-splitting call.

Dressed for Dinner

Penguins walk very upright on land because their feet are set so far back on their body. This upright position, along with their coloring, makes them look a bit like people in formal evening clothes. The white shirt front and black dinner jacket people sometimes wear resembles the black and white feathers of a penguin. Some cartoonists have drawn people as caricatures of penguins. The most famous example is the Penguin, Batman's criminal arch-enemy.

▲ MACARONI PENGUINS

The Macaroni penguin is the second-largest Crested penguin, after the similar Royal penguin. It is 28 inches high and weighs 11 −13 lbs. There are over 11 million breeding pairs of Macaronis. They are named after a group of men called the Macaroni Club, who wore bright feathers in their caps, and introduced Macaroni pasta to England.

▼ TWIN MOHICAN

Named after its stubby, upright crest, the Erect-crested penguin breeds on islands around southern New Zealand. The total population is fairly small— around 200,000 pairs. With a length of 26 inches and a weight of 9−11 lbs., Erect-crested penguins are larger than Snares or Fjordland penguins, but are generally less aggressive.

SURLY ROCKHOPPER ▶

The most aggressive of all penguins, Rockhoppers are named after their habit of bounding over rocks with both feet together. They often jump feetfirst into the water, unlike other penguins, which prefer to walk or dive. Rockhoppers are the smallest of the Crested penguins, with red eyes and a drooping yellow crest. The total breeding population of about 3.7 million pairs nests on islands around Antarctica in the Indian and Atlantic Oceans.

Divers and Ringed Penguins

◄ BIG KING

King penguins are the second-largest penguins after the Emperor. They can weigh up to 31 lbs. King penguins look like Emperor penguins, but have a brighter yellow bib. Their bills open wider than those of any other penguin, allowing them to eat bigger prey. During the day, King penguins make deep dives down to 1,000 feet. There are more than a million pairs of King penguins breeding on subantarctic and Antarctic Islands.

The penguins on these pages are either Diving or Ringed penguins. The largest Diving penguins are the King and Emperor. They have their own genus, as do the Little penguin and its close relative the White-flippered penguin. The Yellow-eyed penguin of New Zealand is the only member of the third Diving penguin genus. All Ringed penguins belong to one genus. Ringed penguins have ring-shaped bands of black and white on their chest and head. They are also called the warm-weather group, because they live in warmer places than other penguins.

▼ SMALLEST SPECIES

The smallest of all the penguins, the Little penguin, is also called the Blue, or Fairy, penguin. Little penguins live in southern Australia and New Zealand. They are smaller than many types of duck and weigh 2–4 lbs.

▲ SHY RARITY

The rarest of all the penguins, the Yellow-eyed penguin breeds on the southeast coast of New Zealand. This penguin is the third tallest, after the Emperor and King penguins. Unlike most other penguins, it is very shy and will not come ashore if people are around.

◀ PORTUGUESE DISCOVERY

The Magellanic penguin was named after the Portuguese explorer, Ferdinand Magellan, who was the first to report its existence in 1519. It is the only Ringed penguin to have two complete black bands across its chest. Magellanic penguins breed from the coast of Argentina, around the tip of South America to southern Chile, as well as on the Falkland Islands. The world population is probably between one and two million birds.

HUMBOLDT PENGUINS ▼

Sometimes called the Peruvian penguin, the Humboldt penguin breeds along the coasts of Chile and Peru, where the cool Humboldt current creates rich fishing grounds. (The Humboldt current was named after the German geographer, Alexander von Humboldt.) Humboldt penguins are probably the least studied of all the penguins in the wild, even though they live near people. They are endangered, mostly due to humans interfering, and fewer than 10,000 are thought to remain.

▼ AFRICAN JACKASS

African penguins are also called Black-footed penguins, because their feet are black, or Jackass penguins, because their call sounds like a jackass or donkey braying. This is the only penguin commonly found in Africa. It lives in cool water currents off the southern African coast. In the last hundred years, numbers of African penguins have gone down from more than one million birds to about 16,000, due to egg collection, pollution, and intensive fishing.

LIFE IN THE TROPICS ▼

The Galapagos penguin, the smallest of the Ringed penguins, lives only on the hot Galapagos Islands, off the western coast of South America. It survives so close to the equator because of a cool water current that washes past the islands. Temperatures in the Galapagos may exceed 104°F, so Galapagos penguins spend the day in the water, only coming onto land at night, when it is cooler.

The World's

Imagine a penguin that weighs no more than a bag of sugar. That is how much the world's smallest penguin, the Little penguin, weighs. Although the Little penguin is small, it is quite fierce and will bite an attacker and fight with its flippers. Little penguins breed in colonies near the shore and stay in their colonies all year long. They nest underground, so total numbers are difficult to count, but there are several hundred thousand birds in Australia. On southeastern Australia's Phillip Island, Little penguins have been studied since 1967. Half a million tourists visit them every year.

NIGHT BIRDS

The Little penguin goes in and comes out of the sea only under the cover of darkness, perhaps to avoid predators. When it starts getting dark, the penguins gather in large rafts near the shore. Then, at dusk, they come on to land. They spend the night in burrows and other caves. Nesting penguins stay in their burrows all day, too.

BODY BASICS

Unlike most penguins, the Little penguin has no crests or colors on its head. Its eyes are gray or hazel, and its bill is black. It has a more stooped posture than the other penguin species and often looks as if it is about to topple over.

SWIMMING STYLE

At sea, the Little penguin lies low in the water, often in small groups. When it swims, it comes to the surface to breathe and then dives down again. The Little penguin usually catches prey by diving down to depths of less than 50 feet. It catches and swallows small fish under the water, but brings large fish to the surface and then swallows them.

Smallest Penguin

ON GUARD

Both parents feed and guard the chicks until they are eight or nine weeks old and ready to go out to sea on their own. The chicks beg for food greedily, often almost knocking over their parents as they clamor noisily for their meal.

UNDERGROUND NESTS

Little penguins nest in burrows, most often using natural holes or gaps under rocks, bushes, and buildings. They may nest under railway tracks or in caves. If necessary, pairs of penguins dig a shallow burrow together in sandy soil, using their bills and feet. Nests are usually 3–6 feet apart and lined with plant material and seaweed. Both parents sit on the eggs for 36 days to keep them warm.

FLUFFY CHICKS

Little penguins usually lay one clutch of two eggs every year. The newborn chicks are covered in gray, fluffy down, but soon grow a second coat of brown, fluffy feathers. They grow rapidly, reaching their adult weight in four to five weeks.

How the Body Works

Beneath a penguin's feathers is a thick layer of fatty blubber, which keeps it warm and stores energy. Energy stores are particularly important to penguins because they have to go for long periods without food while they look after their eggs and chicks, and when molting their feathers on land. A penguin's bony skeleton supports and protects its internal organs, such as the heart and lungs. The bones are solid and heavy, helping penguins to dive under the water. (Flying birds have hollow bones to reduce their weight.) The bones inside the flipper are wide and flat, to push the water aside as the penguin swims. The breastbone has a strong ridge, to which the powerful flipper muscles are attached.

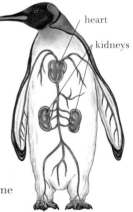

▲ COLD COMFORT
Like all birds, penguins are warm-blooded. They keep their body temperature at a warm 100°F or so, no matter how cold or hot it is around them. To help them keep warm, penguins rely on their dense, overlapping feathers and a thick layer of fat, or blubber, beneath the skin. Blubber is a bad conductor of heat, so it stops the bird's body heat from leaking out into the air.

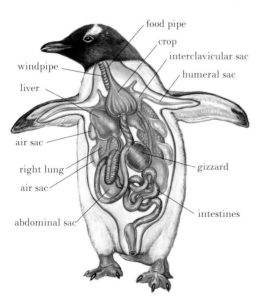

food pipe
crop
interclavicular sac
windpipe
humeral sac
liver
air sac
right lung
gizzard
air sac
abdominal sac
intestines

◄ INSIDE A PENGUIN ▼
These two diagrams show the internal organs of a typical penguin. The one on the left shows the breathing system and the digestive system. The diagram on the right shows the position of the penguin's heart and kidneys, along with some of its blood vessels.

heart
kidneys

HAPPY LANDINGS ▶

Penguins that live in colder places have longer
feathers and thicker blubber than those in
warmer places. Emperor penguins live in the
coldest places of all and are particularly
chubby. Their fatty blubber is useful as a
shock absorber when they leap out of the
sea onto land. It also serves as an energy
store, useful when the Emperors are caring
for their eggs and chicks and cannot get
back to the sea to feed. The large size of
Emperors helps them to stay warm, because
they have a smaller surface area compared
to their body volume than a smaller penguin.

◀ AIR TRAVEL

When penguins are traveling to
and from their feeding grounds,
most swim like dolphins and
porpoises, plunging in and out
of the sea. This behavior, called
"porpoising," lets the penguins
breathe without stopping and
may help confuse predators.
Porpoising may help penguins to
travel faster, since there is less
drag in the air to hold them back
than there is under the water.

SALTY SOLUTION ▶

Penguins can drink sea water, because
they have special glands in their bills
that help get rid of extra salt from the
blood. The glands produce a salty
liquid, which is more salty than sea
water and drips out of the nose. Salty
droplets often collect at the tip of the
bill, and the penguins shake them off,
as this Adélie penguin is doing. Many
other seabirds, including gulls,
cormorants, shearwaters, and petrels,
also have these salt glands.

Fantastic Feathers

Like all birds, penguins are covered in feathers, but their feathers look very different from those of other birds. Penguins' feathers are small, stiff structures that look more like fur or scales, and are tightly packed above a layer of fine down. This arrangement means that they are smooth and waterproof on top to make swimming easier, but warm underneath to stop the penguin from getting cold. Penguins preen their own feathers and each other's to keep them in good condition. They spend hours a day preening, especially when they leave the water.

▲ THERMAL PADDING
A penguin's feathers are very stiff and turn at the tip. They have a fluffy outgrowth near the base, which creates a double layer of protection for the skin that is like a fluffy comforter with an undershirt on top. The fluffy base of the feathers stops body heat from escaping, and the outer "shirt" stops wind blowing warmth away from the body. If penguins need to cool down, they ruffle and separate feathers to allow heat to escape.

◄ WASH AND BRUSH
Penguins must look after their feathers so that they stay waterproof and keep out the cold. To preen its feathers, a penguin spreads oil over them with its bill. The oil comes from a preen gland at the base of the tail. A penguin also uses its bill to tidy its feathers.

▼ YOU SCRATCH MY BACK…

Some species, such as Rockhoppers, preen each other's feathers. This is called allopreening, and it occurs between males and females, as well as between penguins of the same sex. Allopreening helps penguins to remove parasites, such as ticks, and is important in strengthening pair bonds.

▲ FLUFFY CHICKS

When young penguins hatch, they are covered with warm, downy feathers that make them look very different from the adults. As the chicks grow up, the fluffy down is soon replaced by true feathers.

▼ FINE NEW FEATHERS

While penguins are growing new feathers, they have to stay on land and cannot feed. Penguins need lots of energy to grow new feathers so, before they molt, they spend weeks at sea feeding and storing energy in the form of fat. New feathers start to grow under the skin while the penguins are still at sea. After they come ashore to molt, the new feathers push out the old ones.

▲ CHECKING THE RUDDER

On land, penguins use their short, stubby tail feathers to prop themselves upright and help them keep their balance when bending backward to preen their feathers. Under the water, the short, stubby tail makes a useful rudder to help with the steering.

15

Different Colors

Most penguins have black backs and white fronts, except for the Little penguin, which has a dark blue back and a white front. Other sea creatures, such as killer whales and sharks, are also dark on top and light underneath. This "countershading" helps penguins and other creatures to blend in with their environment so they can catch prey and avoid predators. When penguins are on land, their black back helps them to soak up the sun's warmth and their white front reflects heat away from them. From the chest up, each species has different colors, skin patterns, and crests, which help them to recognize each other and are also used for display and courtship.

ALL BLACK AND WHITE
These Adélie penguins show the clear difference between a penguin's black back and white front. These colors help to camouflage the penguin in the water. To a predator or prey looking upward, the white belly is hard to see against white ice on the surface or the lighter sky above the water. Looking down on a penguin, the black back blends better with the dark depths of the sea below.

CHARACTERISTIC "HELMET"
Chinstrap penguins are very easy to recognize because of the narrow band of black-tipped feathers that extends from ear to ear under their chin. This looks like the strap on an English guardsman's helmet, which is worn under the chin.

and Crests

COLORFUL MAKE-UP

King penguins have a golden-orange ear patch, which extends as a narrow stripe around the sides of the neck to the upper breast. There the color fades downward to yellow and merges with the white of the breast. When King penguins first grow their proper feathers, they are still less colorful than those of adults.

MOVEABLE HEADGEAR

The Erect-crested penguin is the only penguin with a crest that stands up rather than flops down. The crest is very stubby and brushlike, and no part of it comes below the bird's eye level. This species is also the only penguin that can raise and lower its crest. No one knows exactly why Erect-crested penguins do this, although it is probably a way of communicating their mood to others. When young birds first grow their feathers, they have a smaller crest than the adults.

STRIPY FACE

The Yellow-eyed penguin has distinctive face markings as well as an unusual eye color. In the adult, the crown of the head, the sides of the face, and the chin are all pale yellow. Each feather here has a black streak down the middle. There is a broad yellow band that extends from the base of the bill, around the eyes, to the back of the head.

Flightless Wonders

Swift and graceful swimmers and divers, penguins are probably better adapted for life at sea than any other group of birds. They usually travel around 4–5 mph, using their flippers to "fly" underwater, and their tails and feet for steering, and possibly braking. The small size of penguin flippers helps to reduce drag. On the surface, penguins swim slowly with a small flipper stroke. A large stroke would bring the flipper out of the water, and therefore not push the penguin forward very far. Penguins usually stay underwater for only a few minutes at a time.

▲ DIVING CHAMPIONS

The best penguin divers are also the biggest —Emperor penguins. Emperors can dive down over 1,300 feet, although most dives are less than 350 feet. The record dive for an Emperor penguin lasted about 18 minutes.

surface

300 ft.

Chinstrap
penguin

Little penguin

Gentoo penguin

600 ft.

King penguin

900 ft.

1,200 ft.

Emperor penguin

◄ HOW DEEP DO PENGUINS DIVE?

This chart shows the diving depths of five species of penguin. Larger species can dive to greater depths, because they are able to store greater reserves of oxygen to keep their muscles working. King penguins dive underwater for about seven and a half minutes, and medium-sized penguins dive for three to six minutes. Little penguins rarely dive for more than one minute.

◀ JUST AFLOAT

Penguins' bodies are quite dense—they are heavy for their size—so they float very low in the water. If they were less dense (lighter), they would float higher, but would find it hard to push their way under the water and stay below the surface. A penguin's darker colors and markings are only on the top part of the body, partly because this is the part that shows above the surface of the water.

FLIPPER SWIMMING ▶

A penguin's flippers are more like an airplane's wings than those of birds that fly in air. The long, narrow shape gives a strong propelling action in water, which is much denser than air and needs more effort to push through. The weight of a penguin is canceled out in water, so the wings just have to propel it forward.

OUT TO DRY ▼

The flightless cormorants of the Galapagos Islands are the only other sea birds apart from penguins that cannot fly. Their small, ragged wings are too weak for flying and swimming, and they push themselves through the water using their powerful legs and webbed feet. Flightless cormorants hold their wings out to dry their feathers after they have been swimming.

▲ PADDLE STEAMBOAT

Two kinds of South American duck have such short wings that they cannot fly. They are called steamer ducks because of their habit of flapping over the surface of the water with a great deal of spray, like an old-fashioned, paddle steamboat. These diving ducks use their wings and legs to splash across the surface at a speed of over 12 mph.

When they are chased by predators, penguins can swim at speeds of up to 7.5 mph. Did you know?

Waddle, Hop, Slide, and Jump

Although penguins may look clumsy and awkward on land, they are actually quite agile. In addition to waddling around at 2.5–3 mph, they can leap high out of the water and some can jump over rocks. Uphill, penguins use their flippers to help propel themselves. On the snow, they can slide on their fronts like living toboggans. Some penguins walk long distances to reach their breeding colonies. Emperor penguins travel hundreds of miles over the sea ice to reach their breeding sites. Adélie penguins also make long journeys. They cannot wait for the ice to melt and allow them to swim to their nest sites, because the Antarctic summer is so short and there is not much time for breeding. Instead, they walk long distances over the ice, and they are very good at navigating from the angle and position of the sun.

▼ THE LONG MARCH

Long columns of Emperor penguins march from their feeding grounds out at sea to reach their breeding areas. The side-to-side waddle of a penguin may look awkward, but it helps to save energy, like a clock pendulum storing energy at the end of each swing, ready for the next swing. Once Emperor penguin parents have chicks, they must travel to and from the sea to catch food for them.

▲ STANDING UP STRAIGHT

When penguins walk on land, they have to stand up straight, with the weight of the body balanced over the feet. This King penguin is stretching up to make itself very tall, probably to display to another penguin. The short, stubby tail of a penguin is not much use for balance, but it can be used to prop up its body on land.

Race to the Pole

Members of Captain Scott's expedition to the South Pole struggle to pull a heavy sled over the ice. In 1910, Scott planned to be the first person to reach the South Pole, but found polar travel and survival much more difficult than the penguins. His expedition arrived at the Pole only to find that the Norwegian explorer, Roald Amundsen, had reached it weeks before them. Tragically, Scott and four companions—Wilson, Bowers, Oates, and Evans—all died on the journey home.

▲ BOUNCING BACK

As penguins leap out of rough seas onto hard, sharp rocks and ice shelves, their bodies have to withstand many knocks and bangs. Penguins' squishy blubber helps to cushion the landing but their feathers are also tough and their skin is strong and leathery. This helps the birds to avoid injury when they enter and leave the sea.

◄ LOOK BEFORE YOU LEAP

Rockhoppers get their name from the way they jump from rock to rock with both feet held together. These Crested penguins lean forward to look at gaps and work out the distance between rocks before they jump. Rockhopper penguins are a bit like human mountaineers; they have the ability to climb, bound, and claw their way up even steep rocky slopes. Sometimes they use their bill like a third leg to give them a stronger grip on the rock and ice.

TOBOGGAN IN THE SNOW ►

Penguins that live in snowy places often lie down on their chests and slide along. They row themselves with their flippers and push with their feet, or use their feet to act as brakes. In this way, penguins can move faster than they can walk, and can travel faster than a person over short distances.

Eyes, Ears, and Noses

Penguins rely on their senses of sight, hearing, smell, and taste to help them catch food, escape danger, and interact with other penguins. They can see well in both air and water, and they see in color. Like most birds, penguins look forward with both eyes. The view they see with one eye overlaps that seen by the other eye. This is called binocular vision—people have it, too. It helps penguins to judge distances and catch prey. Penguins have good hearing, but their hearing is not as sharp as that of sea mammals, such as dolphins and seals.

penguin eye in air · eye of water creature in air

penguin eye in water · eye of land creature in water

▲ COLORFUL EYES ▶

The colored part of a penguin's eye is called the iris. Many species, such as King penguins (above, middle) have brown eyes. Little penguins (right) have blue-gray eyes. Penguins with brighter eye colors include red-eyed Rockhoppers (above, bottom) and the Yellow-eyeds (top).

▲ GETTING IN FOCUS

Penguins have large eyes with a circular pupil to let in plenty of light. Their eyes are adapted for seeing in both air and water. To see a clear image in air, penguins have strong eye muscles to change the shape of the lens and a relatively flat layer at the front of the eye. This stops their eyes from bending light too much and causing things to look blurred in the distance.

EXTRA EYELID ▶

Penguins, like all birds, have a clear third eyelid called the nictitating membrane, usually held open at the side of the eye. This is sometimes called the blinking membrane and is also found in reptiles, amphibians, and some mammals. Penguins move their third eyelid across the surface of the eye to keep it clean. It also helps to protect the eye from injury.

◀ MAKING A RACKET

The Maoris of New Zealand call the Yellow-eyed penguin "*hoiho*," meaning "noise shouter," after its loud trumpet call. Sound is important to this species, because it nests in dense vegetation and cannot see its neighbors and rivals very easily. Most calling happens in the breeding season and includes the trumpeting of mated pairs at the nest site, a yelling threat or alarm call, and grunting chuckles, which are used as a threat signal.

ODOR DETECTION ▶

Most birds have a poor sense of smell, but a penguin's sense of smell may be good. A large area of the brain is taken up with the matter used to process smells. Humboldt penguins that are kept in captivity have been shown to have a sense of smell. A penguin's nostrils are partway along the top half of its bill, which can clearly be seen in this Jackass penguin.

▲ GRIPPING STUFF

Penguins have efficient weapons with which to deal with their prey. The gristly, backward-pointing spines on the tongue and roof of the mouth, plus the powerful beak, help them to grip slippery, wriggling prey. They can also swallow without fear of drowning. Macaroni penguins may use their bills to stun their prey before they start to eat. Magellanic and Humboldt penguins have sharp, heavy bills, which can wound fish.

Food and Feeding

Penguins are all meat-eaters that feed in cool waters. Some swallow stones to help grind up their food. Penguins feed on three main types of food: small fish, squid, and shrimplike krill, which are rich in vitamins and oils. Some penguins take all three types of prey, while others vary their diet according to where they hunt. King and Emperor penguins dive to deeper levels to feed mainly on squid. Emperors can eat up to 31 lbs. of food at a time. Smaller penguins, such as Adélies, Gentoos, and Chinstraps live mostly on krill, which rise toward the sea's surface at night. Little and African penguins feed more on fish than krill, because there are more fish than krill in the warmer waters where they live.

CHAIN OF LIFE ▶

Penguins are in the middle of the Antarctic marine food chain. Their food chain starts with tiny floating plants, called phytoplankton, which are eaten by tiny animals, such as krill, as well as fishes and squid. Penguins are the next link in the chain, but they themselves are eaten by seals, which in turn are eaten by killer whales, the top predators.

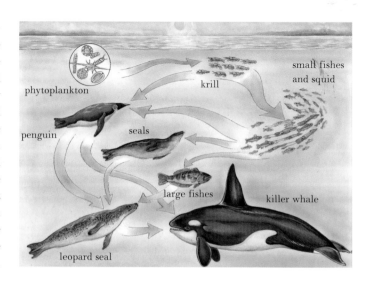

phytoplankton

krill

small fishes and squid

penguin

seals

large fishes

killer whale

leopard seal

▲ I'M HUNGRY

Penguin parents store the food they catch out at sea in their stomachs, then bring up the food to feed their chicks on land. This is called regurgitation. The parent bends over, and the chick puts its head into the parent's mouth to take the food.

▲ THE CHASE IS ON

Penguins, such as these Galapagos penguins, dive underwater to catch their prey. They dart to and fro, grabbing individual fish in mouthfuls of water. Fish are caught sideways and then turned around in the bill to be swallowed headfirst. Some penguins swim in circles around a group of fish to drive them into a dense mass before diving in for the kill.

▲ BIG MOUTH

Humpback whales feed on the same prey as penguins. They use long fringes of baleen that hang from their top jaws to strain krill and fish from the water. When people killed a lot of baleen whales in the nineteenth and early twentieth centuries, more food was left for the penguins, so their numbers increased dramatically.

▲ FEEDING TIME

The correct diet is vital to the survival of penguins in zoos. The smaller species need about 1 lb. of fresh fish daily, whereas the larger Kings and Emperors are fed 2–4.5 lbs. More food is given before the penguins molt.

Attack and Defense

▲ GO AWAY!

Penguins usually have very little space for nesting. They build their nests close together and defend the area around their own nest fiercely. If a strange penguin moves past a nest, the resident makes sure it leaves the nest alone by pecking and waving its flippers.

▲ EGG FOR BREAKFAST

Predatory birds called skuas sometimes steal a penguin's egg if a parent leaves the egg for a moment. Two skuas may attack together, so that while a penguin is chasing one of them, the other skua grabs the egg. Feeding on newly laid eggs is very messy, because skuas cannot pick up the sticky egg white with their bills, only the rich yellow yolk.

Even though they cannot fly, penguins have few natural predators on land, because they usually choose isolated nesting sites. The penguin's beaks and flippers make good weapons, and they use them to attack rivals at nest sites and even scientists trying to study the way they live. On land, penguins are prey to birds such as skuas, which carry off their eggs and chicks. Penguins are most at risk in the water, where they spend most of their lives. Sea predators tend to be mammals, such as seals and killer whales, but sharks also attack penguins.

▼ FIT FIGHTERS

Penguins sometimes have fierce fights with rivals over mates and nest sites. The birds chase each other, making loud squealing noises. They may lock their bills together and hit each other with the hard edges of their flippers. In these fights, nests and chicks may be trampled. In some extreme cases, penguins can kill each other.

▲ DANGER FROM ABOVE

Birds such as skuas hang around penguin colonies looking for weak or sick chicks. Skuas will watch a sick chick for days, not attacking until the youngster is too weak to fight back. Chicks on the edge of a colony are especially at risk. Skuas may even roll a chick outside the colony, where it can be killed out of reach of the adults.

▲ FURRY MENACE

Land mammals are often a big problem for penguins living in warmer places, such as New Zealand. Mammal predators include creatures such as this stoat, as well as ferrets, foxes, dogs, and cats. These animals have been introduced by people to areas where they did not live originally, so the penguins are not adapted to deal with them.

Pick Up a Penguin

Scientists who try to find out more about how penguins live may sometimes be attacked by sharp bills or beating flippers as they try to attach flipper bands or tracking devices. This Adélie penguin obviously does not approve of having its egg marked for a scientific study. Herding the penguins into a temporary corral may sometimes be a useful way of avoiding long chases, which can harm and tire the birds.

▲ SWIMMING LEOPARDS

Near penguin colonies, fast-swimming leopard seals prowl in the water waiting to grab a meal. These sleek predators have a long, flexible neck, a wide mouth, and strong, sharp teeth. They lurk beneath the ledges, where penguins dive into the water, and chase their prey underwater. Then they carry their victims to the surface, where they remove the skin before swallowing.

Penguin Talk

Penguins communicate with calls, as well as behavior patterns called displays. These displays may involve head and flipper waving, bowing, and pointing with the bill. There are three main kinds of penguin calls: contact calls to recognize colony members at sea; display calls between breeding partners; and threat calls to defend nests and chicks, and warn against predators. Males and females have different calls. Calls and displays in the breeding season help penguins to attract mates, recognize partners, and stay together in order to raise the chicks. Penguin communication involves just two individuals at a time, though there may be thousands nesting together.

▲ WARNING DISPLAY

Most penguins are noisy and aggressive, and the majority of species nest in open ground, so threat behavior is very important. When birds do not recognize each other or lay claim to the same nest site, they perform an aggressive display. This acts as a warning, telling rivals to "Get out". If the rival does not take the hint, fighting may follow.

◀ I AM THE GREATEST

All male penguins, except for the Emperor and the Little penguin, advertise themselves with an "ecstatic display." This is their way of saying "I am the greatest, and I am available." This display is used by male penguins to attract a mate. Those with the best displays are most likely to impress females. The ecstatic display incorporates just about everything that a penguin can do. The bill points toward the sky, the flippers beat in a steady rhythm, the eyes roll, and the bird calls loudly. Head feathers may be raised and the bill opened for greater effect. King penguin males and females both use a display like this.

Did you know? The contact call of Emperor and King penguins can be heard ¾ mile away.

▼ THIS IS MY NEST

To lay claim to a nest site out in the open, Gentoos perform a display with simple bowing, head raising movements, and calling. Little penguins do this, too, even though they mainly nest in burrows and crevices. Penguins that always nest in holes do not have displays to claim nest sites, because their nests are better protected from attack.

▲ STRENGTHENING BONDS

A pair of penguins may perform a mutual display together. In Crested penguins such as these Rockhoppers, this involves swinging the head between raised flippers with the bill gaping wildly, after bowing while making loud throbbing sounds. Mutual displays happen just before eggs are laid and when one partner arrives to take over care of the eggs or chicks.

◄ A GIFT FOR THE LADY

This Chinstrap penguin is bringing a stone to his mate to impress her and show that he is serious about bringing up a family. This is part of a whole sequence of displays that leads to a pair of penguins building a nest and rearing a family. First the male advertises that he is ready and drives rivals away, then he brings gifts and sings and bows with the female, and finally, he waits to see if the female accepts or rejects him.

TAKING TURNS TO SPEAK ►

Penguin calls range from the trills and trumpeting of the Emperor and the scratchy cooing of the Adélie, to the harsh braying of the African penguin. When a pair calls together, as these Chinstrap penguins are, they take turns. One bird calls in reply to the other.

Courtship

Most penguins do not breed until they are two to five years old. Once they have traveled to their nest site, they display and call to attract a mate. Most keep the same partner for the whole breeding season. Courtship displays are most complex in penguins that nest in large colonies (such as Adélies, Chinstraps, Gentoos, and Crested penguins) and less complex in penguins that nest in dense vegetation (Yellow-eyed penguins) and in burrows. In many species, males display first to establish a nest site and attract a mate, so the females choose or reject mates, rather than the other way around. A female usually picks her mate from the previous season, unless he fails to return or comes back at a different time.

▲ FEMALE OR MALE?
Female and male penguins usually look alike, and it is difficult to tell them apart. However, in the Crested penguins, such as these Macaronis, the males are larger, more robust, and have bigger bills. During the breeding season, female penguins can sometimes be identified by the muddy footprints the males leave on their backs during mating.

◄ BOW TO YOUR PARTNER
Part of a King penguin's courtship involves a display called "dabbling." Partners stand about 1.5 feet apart, facing each other. One bird drops its head sharply forward, with the bill pointing toward the ground or the partner's feet. The bill may be opened and closed rapidly to make a clapping noise. The bowing bird may also preen its own or its partner's feathers.

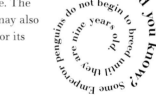

Did you know? Some Emperor penguins do not begin to breed until they are nine years old

▲ AUK COURTSHIP

Little auks display together, both on land and on the water. They also have a special courtship flight, in which the position of the wings and the speed at which they beat are different from normal flying. Eventually, the birds pair up and carry out displays such as the courtship walk, with the male following the female and holding his head down. The auks also face each other and make rapid side-to-side head movements.

▲ OSTRICH DANCE

Male ostriches display to females by squatting and waving their huge black and white wings, one after the other. If the brown females are ready to mate, they lower their head and both wings, and quiver their wings.

▼ BALANCING ACT

When penguins mate, the female lies flat on the ground with her flippers out to the side, and the male climbs on her back in a delicate balancing act. Mating lasts for only two or three seconds. If a male tries to mate with a female and she is unwilling, she stands up so that he falls off her back.

▼ CLOSE COUPLE

A pair of King penguins mate about two to three days after they have settled at a particular site. After a long period of a bowing display called "dabbling," the male either hooks his neck over the female and presses her downward or leans forward against the female's back. The male may also rub the female's neck with his bill. After mating, a King penguin pair may perform some more dabbling displays.

31

The Display

Adélie penguins court each other at their nest sites, which are on rocky islands, beaches, or hill slopes that are free from ice. Breeding colonies contain up to half a million birds. At the end of winter, the breeding pairs return to the same area that they used the previous year, hoping to meet last year's mate at the nest site. If both members of a pair fail to arrive at about the same time, the first penguin may find a new mate. The female chooses her partner. If her previous partner already has a new mate when she arrives, she will try to drive the new mate away. If the female has already mated by the time her old mate arrives, she will go back to her old mate and desert her new one. Adélie penguins pair up with the previous year's mate about 62 percent of the time. The three main courtship displays in Adélies are the ecstatic display, bowing, and the mutual display.

NEST COMMERCIAL

Single males usually perform the ecstatic display to attract a female. The display starts with slow flipper beats, as the Adélie stretches its whole body and points upward with its bill. The neck is inflated, the eyes roll down and backward, the head feathers are raised, and the flippers beat horizontally.

WE HAVE JUST MET

Once a female approaches the nest site, the Adélie pair display together. They arch their necks forward and point their bills at the ground in a deep bow. As they do this, they hold their flippers tightly against their sides and lean forward.

of the Adélies

A SIDEWAYS GLANCE

The bowing display Adélie penguin pairs make when they meet is often interrupted by an aggressive threat display, such as the sideways stare. One of the birds lowers its head and turns one side of its face toward the other bird. The male always raises his head feathers at this point, but the female relaxes or only partly raises her head feathers. The male's bill will be pointed much more toward the female than hers is toward him. The penguin in this picture is giving the sideways stare to a penguin that is getting too close to the nest.

THE FEELING IS MUTUAL

The loud mutual display is usually given by a pair of Adélies at the nest, often in response to the ecstatic display or following mutual bowing. Sometimes it happens after a disturbance in the colony. The birds face each other with their bills open and pointing upward, necks outstretched, eyes rolled down and back, head feathers raised, and flippers held to the sides. Sometimes the penguins sway from side to side and call loudly. In the quiet mutual display, the movements are less obvious, the bills are closed, and the birds are either quiet or call softly.

MATING TIME

When the pair of Adélies are ready to mate, the male bows low to the female as she lies on the nest and approaches her from the side. With his head bent low and flippers beating, he climbs on her back and mates quickly. The male then jumps off the female's back, walks around to the side of the female with his head bowed, and the female flicks her tail forward in jerky movements. Mating happens many times before the eggs are laid.

▲ HEADING HOME

In the Antarctic winter, Adélie penguins stay out at sea feeding. They return to their colonies in September or October. This is the beginning of springtime in the Southern Hemisphere, but there is still a lot of ice around. Adélies may have to travel up to 60 miles from the open water. When they finally reach their colonies, they build nests by scooping out hollows in the ground and lining them with pebbles and sometimes bones.

BACK TOGETHER ▶

Chinstrap penguins breed in large colonies, some of which contain thousands of breeding pairs. Nests are close together, about 2 feet apart. This is not as close as Adélie nests, but closer than Gentoo penguin nests. The best nesting sites are on steep hillsides, where the winter snow melts first. This gives the birds as long as possible to nest and raise their chicks. Nests are made of feathers, stones, and bones, and are large enough to protect eggs from the wind.

Building Nests

Most penguins breed in noisy, smelly colonies. Nesting together helps to protect against predators. The center of a colony is the safest place of all. Both males and females build the nests, using whatever they can find, from seaweed and grass to bones and stones. Stones stop eggs from rolling away and keep them out of the water when snow and ice melt. Penguins may steal nest material from each other, which often causes fights. Most penguins that live in warmer places nest in burrows. Emperor and King penguins do not build nests at all. Instead, they stand upright and keep their eggs on their feet. This means they can move around to find more protected places if they need to. Adélie penguins also hold their eggs on their feet, but lie over them instead of standing up.

▲ MORE NEST MATERIAL

Gentoo penguins often build large nests, usually more than 3 feet apart. If there are no plants around, they will build a nest with pebbles, but when it is possible, they nest among tussock grass. There they make their nests of grass, leaves, twigs, feathers, shells, moss, and pebbles in a scraped-out hollow.

▲ GOING UNDERGROUND

Magellanic penguins often nest in deep burrows with a circular nesting chamber at the end. Both partners help to dig the burrow and build the nest of bones, twigs, pebbles, leaves, and feathers in a little mound at the end. Burrows help to protect the chicks from the sun and from predators.

▼ FOREST PENGUIN

The Fjordland Crested penguin of New Zealand nests in temperate rain forests along the coast, usually less than half a mile from the sea. Nests are well spaced, and one pair of penguins can usually see only about two other pairs. The nests are built of fern fronds, other plant material, and stones, which may be stolen from nearby nests. They are often built in hollows at the foot of trees, underneath boulders, or in small caves.

▼ SOFT GRASS LINING

Rockhopper nests vary from scrapes (shallow dips) in the ground lined with stones, to more elaborate structures made of plant material or bones. In the Falkland Islands, Rockhoppers use nests abandoned by black-browed albatrosses. Some Rockhopper nests may be in caves or behind rocks, but most are in places more exposed to the weather.

Eggs and Hatching

Most penguins lay two eggs, but Emperors and Kings lay only one. One or two young are all that parent penguins can feed. Yellow-eyed penguins lay two eggs of similar size, and experienced adults usually manage to raise two chicks. In Crested penguins, the second egg is much larger and heavier than the first. This is the first egg to hatch—few chicks are hatched and reared from first eggs. In other penguins, apart from Chinstraps, the first egg is usually larger than the second and usually hatches first. The first chick usually survives but the second does not. Except for Emperor penguins, both parents take turns to keep the eggs warm. This is called incubation. While one parent is incubating, the other can be out at sea feeding. Incubation time varies between species, from one to two months.

▲ NICE AND COSY
King penguins hold their single egg on top of their feet to keep it off the cold ground. They cover the egg with a loose fold of skin, like a mitten or muff. Underneath this fold of skin is a swollen patch of skin without any feathers, called a brood patch. Heat from the penguin's blood passes through the skin of the brood patch to keep the egg warm.

SURVIVAL OF THE BIGGEST ▶
Gentoo penguins lay two eggs. The first egg is laid about three days before the second one and is often larger. It usually hatches first so that the first chick feeds and is already established by the time the second egg hatches. The second chick may not be able to compete with the first chick for food— once they reach a certain age, chicks have to chase their parents to be fed. If there is a food shortage, the smaller chick starves.

◄ KING CHICK

King penguin chicks are covered with sparse down when they hatch. By the end of three weeks, this has been replaced by a thick, brown down, with light gray down on the face and neck. Both parents share the job of keeping the chick warm. It stands on their feet for about seven weeks, until it can control its own body temperature. It takes King penguins about 15 months to rear just one chick, so most breed only once every two years.

Did you know? The second egg of the Macaroni penguin is 71 percent heavier than the first.

CHIPPING THE EGG ►

This Chinstrap penguin chick has made a small hole in the eggshell by chipping it with a sharp bump called an "egg tooth" on the tip of its bill. Chicks call from inside the egg when they are ready to hatch. Penguin chicks may take up to three days to chip their way out of their eggs. Parent birds wait next to the egg, keeping it warm and helping the chick to struggle free.

▼ FREE AT LAST

The newly hatched chick will depend on its parents to keep it warm for about three weeks, by which time it will have grown a second, thicker, downy coat. One parent goes out to sea to get food for the chick while the other stands guard. The guarding parent has to go without food while it waits for its mate to return. It may lose one-third of its weight in this time.

▲ PATIENT PARENT

An Adélie penguin bends down to check its egg, which has started to hatch. Chicks first poke a small hole in the eggshell. They then chip at the shell until they can push off the top. This process can take a long time, and the penguin parent waits patiently, keeping its hatching egg warm and protecting it from predators. Finally, a small, fluffy chick emerges from the shell.

The Life

ICE TREK

Emperor penguins walk long distances across the sea ice to reach their breeding colonies, sometimes over 100 miles from the sea. No one knows how they navigate in the gale-force winds without much daylight. One explanation for how they get back to the sea is that they follow the reflection of water on the clouds.

EXTREME SURVIVORS

As soon as the female lays her egg, the male scoops it up and places it on his feet. Here it stays until it is ready to hatch. The males huddle together through the icy winter, and rely on their dense feathers and fatty blubber to keep them warm. The huddle shuffles slowly around as the males take turns on the edges, where it is coldest.

Emperor penguins breed throughout the Antarctic winter, surviving the harshest weather in the world. This allows the chicks to become independent in the spring, when there is plenty of food. In March (fall in the Southern Hemisphere), the Emperors walk to their breeding colonies on the sea ice around Antarctica. The female lays her egg in May and then goes back to sea to feed, leaving the male to incubate the egg through the winter. Soon after the egg hatches in July, the female returns to care for the chick, and the male heads out to sea to feed again. After a fast of over 15 weeks, he has lost half his weight.

KEEPING WARM

Next to a parent's brood patch, temperatures may be 145°F higher than outside. The male keeps the chick warm for 10 days after hatching, then the female takes over. Young chicks exposed to the icy weather conditions for more than about two minutes will die.

HUDDLED TOGETHER

Emperor chicks form groups, called crèches, at 45 to 50 days old. In the crèche, chicks huddle together for warmth and protection. The Emperor chicks listen for their parents' calls when they return with food. Parents find their own chicks from their high-pitched squealing calls. Emperors recognize their own chicks and are not willing to feed others.

MASK MARKING

Chicks in crèches have a coat of gray down. The face is like a mask, with white circles around the eyes. A rim of black runs from above the eye, down the side of the neck. These markings are different from those of other young penguins, and may help parents find their chicks in the Antarctic darkness.

FEED ME NOW

Emperor penguin parents only manage to feed their chick about 12 to 24 times altogether, but each meal may be as much as 30 percent of the chick's weight. Chicks get more feeds as they grow older, because the ice melts, bringing the open sea full of food closer to the colony.

Early Days

Young penguins are a very different color and pattern from the adults. This probably helps to protect them in the colonies, because adults do not see them as competitors for mates and nesting sites. They do not need to be camouflaged from enemies, because they nest in remote areas, usually with large numbers of other penguins around to keep them safe. Duties, such as feeding and guarding, are usually performed by both parents equally, except in Crested penguins where the male stands guard and the female brings food for the chick. Parents also spend some time grooming their young, which may distract the young from constantly begging for food.

▲ SAFE AND WARM

For the first two to four weeks of their lives, penguin chicks rely on their parents for warmth and protection. Emperor penguin chicks seem especially snug, tucked safely away on the feet of the adults.

◄ ALWAYS HUNGRY`

By the time they are two or three weeks old, young penguins have grown a thick coat of brown or gray down. They look like giant balls of fluff with big feet and small heads, and quickly become almost as large as their parents. Because of this growth, penguin chicks are always hungry. Their parents have to work very hard catching food in the sea and bringing it back for them to eat.

▼ SKUA ATTACK

Young penguins are more at risk from predators than adults, but adults defend their eggs and young fiercely. Predators patrol the colonies on the look out for chicks on their own. If a parent leaves its chick for just a few minutes, predators are always ready to pounce.

▲ MEAL TIME

Newly hatched chicks beg for food by stretching their heads upward, waving them around and giving shrill, piping calls. Older chicks, such as this one, peck at their parents' bills. The chick pushes its bill into the parent's mouth, and the parent brings up food from its stomach. Chicks of large species may eat over 2 lbs. at a time.

Batman and the Penguin

The archenemy of Batman, the Penguin, has appeared in comics, movies, and on television since 1941. His real name is Oswald Cobblepot, and he was born with a short, wobbly body, a birdlike nose, and a bad temper. His rich parents dumped their ugly and deformed baby, but he was adopted by a flock of penguins in Gotham City Zoo. In the 1992 film Batman Returns, *Danny De Vito plays the grown-up Penguin.*

▲ LEAVING HOME

When chicks have grown all their feathers, they are said to have fledged. They can then leave the colony to swim in the sea. Parents do not go with their fledged chicks, so the youngsters have to be able to look after themselves. Young penguins stay at sea for the first few years of their life. Penguins live from 6 to 20 years.

▼ CHANGING CLOTHES

Fluffy down feathers are not waterproof, and chicks cannot go into the water until they have grown their waterproof adult feathers. It takes only seven weeks for Adélie chicks to lose their down, but King penguin chicks may stay fluffy for up to 13 months. While their adult feathers are pushing through the skin, young penguins, like this Erect-crested, look ragged and untidy.

Where Penguins Live

Penguins live only in the southern half of the world, where cold water currents carry nutrients along the coasts of South America, southern Africa, Australia, New Zealand, and the Falkland Islands. Four species—Emperor, Adélie, Gentoo, and Chinstrap penguins—breed on the Antarctic continent, but more than half of all penguin species never visit Antarctica at all. The greatest variety of penguins live on the mainland and islands of southern New Zealand and the Falkland Islands.

▲ THE ICE PENGUINS

Emperor penguins are truly the penguins of ice and snow. They live within the ice that floats around Antarctica and usually avoid the open waters beyond it. Sometimes they dive into seal holes or cracks in the ice to feed. Even their breeding colonies are usually on the ice.

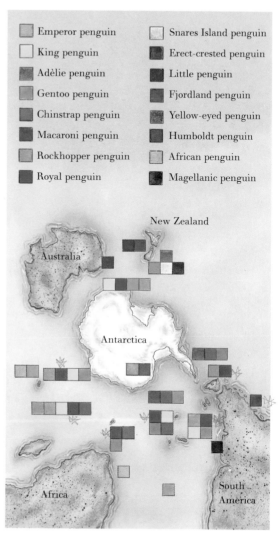

- Emperor penguin
- King penguin
- Adélie penguin
- Gentoo penguin
- Chinstrap penguin
- Macaroni penguin
- Rockhopper penguin
- Royal penguin
- Snares Island penguin
- Erect-crested penguin
- Little penguin
- Fjordland penguin
- Yellow-eyed penguin
- Humboldt penguin
- African penguin
- Magellanic penguin

New Zealand
Australia
Antarctica
Africa
South America

▲ SOUTH OF THE EQUATOR

Penguins are found on every continent in the Southern Hemisphere, and each continent has its own unique species. Penguins may have originally spread from the area around New Zealand, gradually moving south toward Antarctica and north toward the Equator.

42

◀ A PLACE OF THEIR OWN

Royal penguins are found only on Macquarie Island, which is in the Southern Ocean between New Zealand and Antarctica. Here they nest among the lush, tussock grasses, using the same areas every year. Royal penguins are very similar to Macaronis, but have white feathers on their face and throat.

▼ DRY ROCK

Humboldt penguins live along the dry coasts of Peru and Chile. They nest on rocky shores, in sea caves, and among boulders. The Humboldt penguin range overlaps that of Magellanic penguins by nearly 200 miles. Usually, the two species breed in separate colonies.

▲ AT HOME ON THE BEACH

The African, or Jackass, penguin lives only in the coastal waters around southern Africa. It breeds on the mainland and offshore islands, and stays in the same area out of the breeding season. Most African penguins do not go farther than 8 miles from land.

SOME LIKE IT HOT ▼

The Galapagos penguin is a most unusual penguin, breeding on the hot desert islands of the Galapagos. It lives only on these islands and nowhere else in the world. Both adults and young remain at their breeding sites throughout much of the year and do not travel away from the islands.

Warming Up, Cooling Down

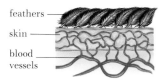

feathers

skin

blood
vessels

normal temperature—feathers lying
down and narrow blood vessels.

high temperature—feathers ruffled
and wide blood vessels near skin surface.

▲ HOT AND COLD

Penguins cannot cool down
by sweating. Instead, they
open blood vessels near the
surface of their flippers, feet,
and face, and ruffle their
feathers to let heat escape.

▼ THICK COAT OF FEATHERS

Adélie penguins must survive temperatures
below freezing. They need to stay active in the
water to generate body heat, which helps them
to keep warm. Adélies have lots of long
feathers, which hold a thicker layer of warm air
close to the skin than those of other penguins.

From the tropical heat of the Galapagos to the
bitter cold of Antarctica, penguins have to work
hard to keep their temperature steady. Like all
birds, they generate their own heat instead of
relying on the sun to warm them up. Fatty
blubber and air trapped by a penguin's feathers
help to keep warmth in. Penguins can also
shiver to create heat, hold their flippers close to
their bodies or huddle together for warmth.
They can even reclaim about 82 percent of the
heat from the air they breathe out through the
nose. Penguins are so good at keeping warm that
they sometimes have trouble with overheating.
Adélies even seem to suffer from the heat if the
temperature gets much above freezing.

▲ COMPLETELY WATERPROOF

A penguin's feathers can be pulled into
different positions by small muscles. On land,
the feathers are raised to trap a thick layer of
air next to the skin, which stops body heat
from escaping. In water, feathers flatten to
form a watertight barrier, forcing out air.

▼ SHADY CHARACTERS

These Magellanic penguins are huddled in the welcome shade of a bush to stay out of the direct sun. They are holding their flippers away from their bodies so they act as radiators to let heat escape. African elephants use their large ears in a similar way to help them cool down.

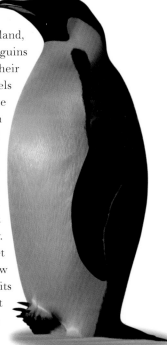

▲ BARE SKIN RADIATORS

Penguins that live in warmer places, such as these African penguins, can lose heat from bare patches on the face, flippers, and feet. These act as radiators, allowing excess body heat to escape into the air, which cools the penguin down.

▼ COOL BURROW

Magellanic penguins nest in burrows, which gives them somewhere private to escape from the heat. It is much cooler underground than out in the hot sun. These penguins go to sea to catch food during the hottest parts of the day, which also helps them to avoid overheating on land.

COLD FEET ▶

When they are resting on land, Emperor and King penguins turn up their feet and put their whole weight on their heels and tail. This reduces the amount of bare skin in contact with the ice and stops the penguin's feet from getting too cold. The way a penguin's blood circulates inside its feet also helps to retain heat inside the penguin's body. It keeps the penguin's feet at around the same low temperature as its surroundings, so it does not lose too much heat through its feet.

45

Penguins

The smallest of the Ringed penguins is also the most extraordinary, and it lives only on the Galapagos Islands. These 19 remote islands are on the Equator, 700 miles west of Ecuador, in South America. Galapagos penguins breed mainly on the coasts of Fernandina and Isabela Islands, usually feeding at sea during the day and returning to the land in the cool of the night. They sometimes come ashore for short periods during the day. Galapagos penguins often show signs of heat stress in the sun. When they are really hot, they pant rapidly. As water evaporates from the tongue, it takes heat away and cools the penguin down.

VOLCANIC HABITAT

The Galapagos Islands are the remains of volcanoes that rose up from the sea bed millions of years ago. The islands consist of jagged, black volcanic rock and dry cactus scrub, a challenging habitat for penguins. They cannot toboggan as penguins living on smooth ice and snow can. Galapagos penguin colonies are always near the sea; in fact, they are never more than 150 feet inland.

OUT IN THE SUN

On land, Galapagos penguins shade their feet with their body to keep them cool. They also hold their flippers out to allow any wind to reach as much of their body as possible, and blow any excess heat away from their body. Heat is lost from the undersides of the flippers and the feet, which are not so heavily insulated with fat and feathers as the rest of the body.

from the Galapagos

A COOL DIP

Galapagos penguins can cool off by swimming in the sea, which is always colder than the land. When they swim on the surface, the penguins hold their flippers under the water, which helps them to keep cool. For the same reason, they rarely leap in and out of the water like porpoises, as other penguins do.

HUNTING FOR A MEAL

The Galapagos penguin eats small fish, such as sardines. It catches prey by diving, but usually stays underwater for less than 30 seconds. There are more fish when the surface waters are cool, and these penguins do not breed unless the water temperatures fall below 75°F.

SIMPLE NEST

Galapagos penguins' nests are usually in shaded places, such as crevices in the rock. They also make simple nest scrapes on the surface, lined with bones, leaves, or feathers. The penguins nest in loose colonies, and each pair can produce up to three clutches a year.

Prehistoric Penguins

It is believed that penguins evolved over 65 million years ago from flying birds that were similar to modern diving petrels, which "fly" underwater. No fossils of anything in between a flying ancestor and a typical penguin have ever been found. There are very few fossils of penguins that have been found, but over 40 different species of fossil penguin have been discovered so far. This means that penguins were once more varied than they are today. The evolution of seals and small whales about 15 million years ago may have contributed to the extinction of large penguins and many of the small ones.

▲ **DID ANCIENT PENGUINS FLY?**
The short answer to this question is yes! Some extinct species have features similar to those of modern albatrosses and petrels, both of which can fly. The modern penguin's flipper bones were modified from a flying wing. Its breastbone has areas for anchoring muscles that were developed originally for flying, and its tail bones have a structure that supports tail feathers in all modern flying birds.

▼ **EXTINCT RECORD-BREAKERS**
Some ancient penguins were much taller and heavier than the Emperor penguin, the largest penguin alive today. The first fossil penguin to be discovered, *Palaeeudyptes antarcticus*, was about 7 inches taller than the Emperor. The two largest fossil penguins discovered so far were much larger than this. *Pachydyptes ponderosus* was up to 22 inches taller than the Emperor penguin. A fossil penguin even smaller than the Little penguin has also been discovered.

6 ft.

6 ft. man   fossil penguin   largest known living penguin   smallest modern penguin   guillemot   Least auklet

mya = millions of years ago

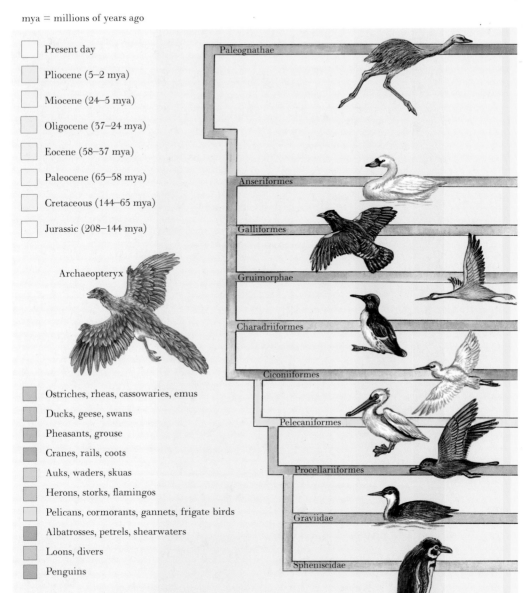

Present day

Pliocene (5–2 mya)

Miocene (24–5 mya)

Oligocene (37–24 mya)

Eocene (58–37 mya)

Paleocene (65–58 mya)

Cretaceous (144–65 mya)

Jurassic (208–144 mya)

Archaeopteryx

Paleognathae

Anseriformes

Galliformes

Gruimorphae

Charadriiformes

Ciconiiformes

Pelecaniformes

Procellariiformes

Graviidae

Spheniscidae

Ostriches, rheas, cassowaries, emus

Ducks, geese, swans

Pheasants, grouse

Cranes, rails, coots

Auks, waders, skuas

Herons, storks, flamingos

Pelicans, cormorants, gannets, frigate birds

Albatrosses, petrels, shearwaters

Loons, divers

Penguins

▲ CHARTING PENGUIN EVOLUTION

This chart shows how penguins may have evolved from ancient shearwaters, petrels, and albatrosses. Divers and loons probably evolved from the same ancestors but they form a separate group from penguins. Penguins, divers, and loons are more closely related to the shearwaters and petrels, from which they descended directly, than they are to each other.

49

Living Relatives

Most scientists today think that penguins are most closely related to flying sea birds called tubenoses, which include shearwaters and petrels. Young Little penguins even develop tubelike openings in their nostrils, just like those that adult tubenoses have. Albatrosses, which are also in the tubenose group, have noisy courtship displays similar to those of penguins. Diving petrels "fly" underwater to chase prey, just as penguins do. When they have molted their feathers, they cannot fly through the air, but they can still fly very well under the water, like penguins. For the part of the year when they are molting, diving petrels live very much like penguins, since they cannot fly. Penguin ancestors probably passed through a stage like this when they were evolving. Apart from petrels and other tubenoses, more distant living relatives of penguins include loons (also called divers), grebes, and frigate birds.

▲ **PADDLING PETRELS**
Cape petrels (also called Cape pigeons or Pintado petrels) usually feed on the surface of the oceans. They paddle their feet in the water to bring plankton to the surface and peck from side to side. Cape petrels also dive for fish and squid, both from the surface and from the air.

Did you know? Diving petrels nest in huge colonies, just like penguins do.

A LIFE ON THE OCEAN WAVES ▶

Shearwaters glide over the sea on long wings, but also dive to catch fish and squid. They use their wings to push themselves underwater and are well adapted for fast swimming. They have strong, streamlined legs, large webbed feet, and compact feathers that allow them to sink more easily. Many shearwaters feed in dim light or at night like some penguins do. Some fossil penguin bones show features that are very similar to those of shearwaters.

▲ COURTING GREBES

Both grebes and penguins may use nest material in their courtship displays. The weed ceremony of these Great crested grebes is part of a complex sequence of displays. Grebes are well adapted to underwater hunting. A diving grebe can move at about 6 feet a second and turn very quickly.

▼ IN ITS ELEMENT

After penguins, loons (or divers) are the most specialized diving birds. They are so well adapted for swimming and diving that they cannot walk properly on land. Unlike penguins, loons use their feet, rather than their wings, to push themselves through the water. They usually hunt fish within 30 feet or so of the surface. Loon chicks can dive just a day after hatching.

▲ SUPER SWIMMER

Seals are not related to penguins—they are mammals, and penguins are birds. But seals are a similar shape because they, too, are adapted for swimming fast underwater. Seals and penguins both have streamlined, torpedo-shaped bodies. Sea lions even use their front flippers for swimming, although true seals, such as this crab-eater, use their back flippers.

▼ AERIAL PIRATE

This male frigate bird has puffed out his throat like a red balloon in order to attract a mate. In the air, frigate birds are agile and acrobatic fliers, plucking fish and squid from near the surface. As well as catching their own food, these large birds steal the prey of others. They chase seabirds and dive-bomb them to force them into dropping what they have caught. Frigate birds are such good fliers that they can even grab the falling fish from the air.

Speedy Sprinters

The best known flightless birds, apart from penguins, are rheas, ostriches, emus, and cassowaries. These are all big birds with long legs, which can run fast over the ground. They do not need to fly to escape danger, because they can run away instead. They all have large, powerful feet to push themselves along. They also use their feet as weapons to defend themselves. Cassowaries, rheas, and emus are also strong swimmers. Even though they cannot fly, these birds do have wings. They may use their wings to help them cool down on hot days, or display them during courtship. Male ostriches, rheas, emus, and cassowaries all play an important role in raising the young.

▲ RARE RUNNER

The ostrich is the biggest bird in the world. It is much too heavy to fly, but it is a fantastic runner. Ostriches can sprint at a speed of up to 45 mph—that is as fast as a car. At high speed, both feet rise up off the ground at once.

▲ RESPONSIBLE FATHER

South American rheas can sprint faster than a horse. They are smaller than ostriches and have three toes on each foot, instead of just two. Male rheas build the nest and look after the eggs and chicks. They may incubate up to 60 eggs at once. Females lay their eggs in the nests of several different males.

▲ HOW MANY TOES?

Ostriches have just two toes on each foot; most other birds have at least three. An ostrich's toes are strong and end in thick, curved claws. They help the ostrich grip the ground when it runs, and help it to kick predators, such as lions.

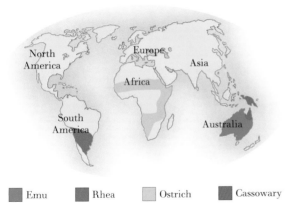

Emu Rhea Ostrich Cassowary

▲ SEPARATE HOMELANDS

Ostriches, rheas, and emus live in different continents. Rheas live only in South America, ostriches in Africa, and emus in Australia. They have all adapted to similar habitats and may share ancestors that lived together when all the continents in the Southern Hemisphere were connected about 150 million years ago.

▲ PROTECTIVE PARENT

The male emu does all the work when it comes to looking after the eggs and chicks. At eight weeks, the eggs hatch and the male becomes very aggressive, attacking anything that comes too close.

Feather Headdress

The people of Papua New Guinea keep all three species of cassowary in captivity and often treat them as pets. They pluck the feathers to use in ceremonial headdresses like this one. Some also use the feather quills for nose decoration. The feathers are part of costumes worn for special occasions concerned with the religious beliefs of the people. Dances are performed to respect the spirits of the ancestors. Cassowaries have been traded by people throughout far Southeast Asia for over 500 years.

▲ BIG BIRD

Cassowaries can be the same height and weight as a person. They live in rain forests in Papua New Guinea and Australia. The cassowary's long, hairlike feathers help to protect its body and keep its skin from getting scratched. Its powerful legs end in daggerlike claws. These birds attack people if they feel threatened.

53

New Zealand's Flightless Birds

The world's most unusual collection of flightless birds live on the islands of New Zealand, about 1,000 miles southeast of Australia. These birds include the unique kiwi, which is related to ostrich, emu, rhea, and the cassowary. New Zealand's other flightless birds are versions of birds that can fly in other places. These birds gave up flying in New Zealand because there were no land predators to fly away from. Unfortunately, people have introduced mammal predators, such as stoats, to New Zealand. These predators find it very easy to catch the flightless birds, and eat their eggs and chicks. Numbers have declined dramatically, and many of New Zealand's flightless birds are now rare.

▲ SNIFFING OUT A MEAL

Kiwis behave more like furry mammals than birds. Even their thick, shaggy feathers look furry. They help to protect the chicken-sized birds from thorny bushes in the forest. Kiwis come out at night and sniff out food with sensitive nostrils at the tip of their long, curved bill. It is rare for a bird to have such a good sense of smell. Although their eyes are small for a nocturnal creature, kiwis can see well enough to run fast through dense undergrowth at night.

GROUNDED ▶

The kakapo is the world's largest parrot and the only one that cannot fly. It has a thick layer of insulating fat under its skin, which makes up about 40 percent of its body weight, and is too heavy to get airborne. Kakapos live on the ground and come out at night. Their green feathers help to camouflage them among the ferns and other forest plants. Kakapos evolved at a time when there were no ground predators in New Zealand to attack them and eat their eggs, so there was no need to fly.

▲ FLIGHTLESS PHOENIX

A century ago, people thought that the takahe, a large, flightless rail, was extinct. But in 1948, it was rediscovered living in remote alpine grassland in the southwest of New Zealand's South Island. Its story is a bit like that of the mythical phoenix, which catches fire and disappears, only to come alive again from the ashes.

▲ MIXED BLESSING

The weka cannot fly. Instead, it uses its wings to help keep its balance as it walks. Wekas are large, flightless rails, with powerful feet and strong claws. They have a varied diet, from grass, seeds, and fruit, to mice, birds, eggs, and beetles. Wekas can be fierce predators of other ground-living birds and have caused serious problems on some islands where they have been introduced. However, they are very good at killing rats that attack other flightless birds.

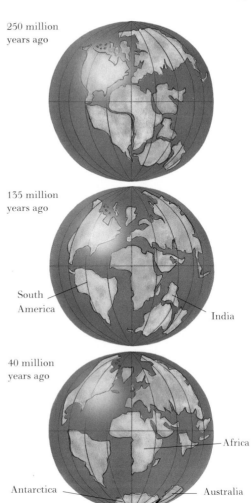

250 million years ago

135 million years ago

South America

India

40 million years ago

Africa

Antarctica

Australia

▲ DRIFTING APART

The islands now called New Zealand were once part of a supercontinent called Gondwanaland, which also included South America, Africa, India, Australia and Antarctica. Gondwanaland began breaking apart 180–140 million years ago. Australia and New Zealand separated from Antarctica and moved away around 100 million years ago. New Zealand finally drifted away from the east coast of Australia about 80 million years ago and has been isolated since.

55

Threats to Penguins

The greatest danger to penguins comes from people. People have polluted the oceans where penguins swim, not only with oil, but also with plastic rubbish that can trap and kill penguins. People have also destroyed the natural habitat of some penguins on land and overfished the seas where penguins feed. Humboldt penguins are accidentally killed in fishermen's nets. In some places, predators introduced by people, such as cats, rats, and ferrets, eat penguin eggs and chicks. In the past, people collected penguin eggs to eat and killed adult birds for their meat, skins, feathers, and the oil in their fatty blubber.

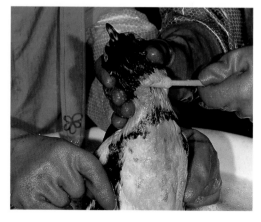

▲ **COMING CLEAN**

Oil spills from tankers and boats cleaning out their engines at sea have a disastrous effect on penguins. The oil mats their feathers, allowing water to get in. Without a layer of warm air near the skin, penguins die from the cold. If they do reach the shore, the oiled birds try to preen their feathers and end up swallowing some of the poisonous oil. This oiled Jackass penguin is being washed carefully after an oil spill off of South Africa.

DUG INTO DUNG ▶

Over 2,000 years ago, the Incas of South America used penguin droppings to make the soil rich and help them grow their crops. The Inca word for this naturally dried fertilizer is "guano." The Incas were careful to harvest guano at a slower rate than the birds produced it, so the supply did not run out. The guano harvested was over 150 feet deep in places. Today, the Humboldt penguin is threatened by overharvesting of guano. There is not enough guano left in which these penguins can dig their nesting burrows. Similar damage in South Africa has been recognized, and action taken to stop any further deterioration of habitat.

◄ PRESSURE FROM PEOPLE

Many people want to see penguins up close, but if this is not properly controlled, it can seriously disturb the birds and cause their numbers to drop. Low-flying helicopters cause great distress to penguins. Parents may even flee from the nest, exposing eggs and chicks to predators. Disturbance drains a parent's energy reserves, which are already low as a result of nesting and molting. Stressed penguins cannot look after and feed their chicks properly, and many chicks die.

DWINDLING FOOD SUPPLY ►

These shrimplike creatures are krill, an important food item in the diet of many penguins. The amount of krill in the sea is affected by the temperature of the water and the amount of ultraviolet radiation from the sun. Changes in these two factors caused by pollution have already cut down the amount of plant plankton, which the krill eat. If there is less krill, then penguins starve.

Did you know? In June 1994, around 40,000 penguins were affected by an oil spill off South Africa.

▼ HEAVY HOOVES

This sheep grazing peacefully among Gentoo penguins does not look as if it is causing any damage. However, sheep are heavy animals and they trample penguin burrows and nests as they walk around. Other introduced animals, such as dogs, cats, and weasels, are predators that attack the penguins directly.

▲ PENGUINS ON THE MENU

Early European expeditions to the Antarctic, such as Captain Cook's expedition (above), slaughtered penguins for their fresh meat. The trusting penguins were easy to kill. Yet this only had a small effect on penguin numbers. Killing penguins for their oil in later decades devastated many colonies, since it took eight penguins to produce just one gallon of oil.

The Timid

The Yellow-eyed penguins breed only around the southeast coast of New Zealand and on the nearby islands of Stewart, Campbell, and Aukland. Adults stay on or near their breeding grounds all year round. These beautiful penguins are endangered on the mainland and rare elsewhere. In the last 40 years, their numbers have dropped by at least 75 percent in some areas. The main reason for this drastic decline is that the forests where the penguins nest have been turned into farms or their trees cut down for timber. More recently, introduced predators, such as cats, pigs, stoats, and ferrets, have begun taking chicks. In some areas, all the chicks may be killed within four weeks of hatching.

WHERE TO NEST?

Now that so much of the coastal forest has been cleared, Yellow-eyed penguins are forced to nest in gullies or on hills, cliff tops, and slopes that face the sea. These nest sites offer no shelter from the hot sun. Yellow-eyed penguins suffer greatly from heat stress, especially during the breeding season. When they are not looking after chicks, they sleep on land in the cool of the night and go to sea by day.

MUSICAL COURTSHIP

This pair of Yellow-eyed penguins are preening each other as part of their courtship display. It helps to keep the pair together by strengthening the bond between them. Yellow-eyed penguins also court with calls. The loud calls of this species are much more musical than the harsh cries of most penguins.

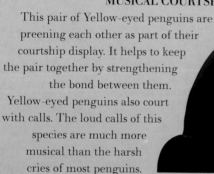

Yellow-eyeds

PRIVATE HIDEAWAY

Yellow-eyed penguin nests are usually well hidden in dense vegetation and scattered over a wide area. These penguins cannot usually see their neighbors, but they can hear them. Both parents build the nest, which is a shallow bowl on the surface made of twigs, grass, leaves, and other vegetation.

CAUGHT BY ACCIDENT

Fishing nets can cause problems for Yellow-eyed penguins. They get tangled up in the nets and drown because they cannot swim up to the surface to breathe. Yellow-eyed penguins seem to be most at risk from nets used for catching bottom-living fish. These nets are set in water that is 300–700 feet deep.

FOREST NURSERY

The natural breeding habitat of the Yellow-eyed penguin is the cool forests along the coast of southeast South Island, New Zealand, and the islands nearby. In the last 140 years, the coastal forests of the mainland have been almost totally destroyed and replaced by farmland.

NESTING BOXES

Conservation groups such as the Yellow-eyed Penguin Trust are working hard to protect Yellow-eyed penguins. They have bought several areas of the penguin's habitat and are replanting them to provide suitable nesting areas. While the conservation groups wait for the plants to grow, large nest boxes placed in suitable areas encourage more penguins to nest, by providing shelter and protection from the heat of the sun.

Protecting Penguins

Penguins are enchanting birds. They have done nothing to harm us, yet we have put many of them at risk. One of the problems about penguin conservation is that we know so little about penguins, especially what happens to them while they are at sea. New technology, such as tracking by satellite, is helping to fill in some of the gaps, but there are still many mysteries to unravel. Penguin habitats on land need to be protected and their breeding colonies kept free of unnecessary disturbance. The captive breeding of rare penguins in zoos and wildlife parks may help these species survive in the future. Cutting back on pollution would help those in the wild.

▲ HABITAT PROTECTION

Penguin nesting areas were first protected in the early 1900s. In 1919, the penguin oil factories on the Macquarie Islands were closed, and the islands were turned into a penguin sanctuary. These tourists are watching penguins on the Macquarie Islands. In 1961, the Antarctic Treaty agreed to protect all penguins, so they could no longer be legally hunted.

FINDING OUT MORE ▶

To help penguins in the future, we need to find out more about how they live. It is difficult to carry out this research without disturbing the penguins, but researchers try to upset them as little as possible. This researcher is collecting data from a Little penguin chick on Kangaroo Island, South Australia. Penguins are weighed and measured, their eggs and chicks are counted, their diet is investigated by flushing out their stomachs with water, and their behavior is carefully observed and recorded. Satellite transmitters are attached to some penguins to help scientists find out where they go and how far they travel during their time at sea.

▲ POPULAR ATTRACTIONS

Penguins did not find their way into most zoos until the nineteenth century, but they are now very popular exhibits. Penguins in zoos help the public to appreciate how beautiful and interesting live penguins are. They are difficult to transport, and it is expensive to create a cold environment that is close to their natural habitat.

▲ ILLEGAL PRACTICE

In some places people have collected penguins' eggs for hundreds of years. In 1897, more than 700,000 African penguin eggs were taken from colonies off the coast of South Africa. Penguin egg collecting was banned in 1969, but in parts of South America, illegal harvesting still continues.

▼ KEEPING A SAFE DISTANCE

Wild penguins are major tourist attractions in New Zealand, southern Australia, South America, and Antarctica. In Antarctica, tourist numbers increased from less than 300 people a year in the 1950s, to more than 5,500 people per year in the early 1990s. At Punta Tombo in Argentina, tourism increased from several dozen people per year in the 1960s, to more than 50,000 per year in the 1990s. Tourists need to be aware of how to behave near penguins, so that disturbance can be kept to a minimum.

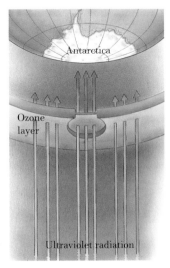

▼ HOLE IN THE SKY

Far up in the atmosphere, 9–56 miles above the Earth's surface, is a layer of a gas called "ozone." Ozone stops harmful ultraviolet rays from reaching the Earth from the Sun. But chemicals, such as CFCs, are causing holes in the ozone layer. The extra ultraviolet radiation coming through the holes damages or kills the microscopic sea creatures on which fish and penguins feed.

Antarctica

Ozone layer

Ultraviolet radiation

GLOSSARY

allopreening
Preening of one bird by another.

baleen
Horny plates that hang down from the top jaw in some whales and are used to filter food from the water.

binocular vision
Type of vision in which both eyes look to the front and have overlapping fields of view.

blubber
The thick layers of fat found under the skin of penguins and sea mammals, such as whales and seals.

breeding season
The time of year when pairs of animals come together to mate and raise a family.

brood patch
A featherless area of thickened skin underneath a bird's body, used to keep eggs warm during incubation.

camouflage
Colors, patterns, or shapes that allow an animal to blend in with its surroundings in order to hide from prey or escape danger.

carnivore
An animal that eats meat.

clutch
The set of eggs laid and incubated together.

colony
A large number of birds that gather together to breed.

conservation
Protecting living things and helping them to survive in the future.

countershading
The coloration of an animal with a dark back and a light underside, which provides camouflage.

courtship
Ritual displays that take place before mating.

crèche
A group of young in the nesting area, which are still dependent on their parents.

down
Fine, fluffy feathers which help to trap air and keep a bird warm. Young chicks only have down.

drag
The resistance to movement in water or air.

ecstatic display
A "stretch up and shout" display, usually given by males during the breeding season. It helps to attract females, drive off rivals, and lay claim to a nest site.

egg tooth
A small, sharp point on the tip of a baby penguin's bill, which helps it to break free from its eggshell.

endangered species
A species that is likely to die out in the near future.

evolution
The process by which living things change gradually over many generations.

flightless
Unable to fly.

flipper
A limb that has been adapted for swimming.

fossils
The preserved remains of animals and plants, usually found in rocks.

genus (plural: genera)
A group of closely related species, such as the Crested penguins.

habitat
The kind of surroundings in which an animal usually lives.

incubation
Sitting on eggs to keep them warm so that baby animals will develop inside.

insulation
Keeping warm things warm and cool things cool.

iris
A thin, colored disc with a hole (the pupil) in the middle. This is on the front of the lens in the eyes of animals with backbones.

keel
A ridge along the breastbone of birds, supporting the powerful flight muscles or swimming muscles. The larger flightless birds do not have this keel.

krill
Small, shrimplike sea creatures that swim in huge shoals.

mammal
An animal with fur or hair and a backbone, that can control its own body temperature. Females feed their young on milk made in mammary glands.

molting
The shedding of old and damaged feathers and the growth of new ones, usually once a year.

mutual display
Interaction between two penguins, usually when they meet at the nest.

navigating
Finding the way to a particular place and following a route.

nictitating membrane
A third eyelid that can be passed over the eye to keep it clean or shield it.

nocturnal
Active at night.

plankton
Tiny creatures that drift with the water movement in the sea or in lakes.

plumage
The covering of feathers on a bird's body.

porpoising
Leaping in and out of the sea's surface, like a dolphin or porpoise.

predator
An animal that catches and kills other animals for food.

preening
The method by which birds care for their feathers, using the bill and oil from the preen gland.

prey
An animal that is hunted and eaten by other animals.

ratites
A group of large, flightless birds, including ostriches, emus, rheas, and cassowaries. Although the ratites belong to different families, they have similar features, such as powerful legs, small wings and no keel on the breastbone.

regurgitate
To cough up food that has already been swallowed, to feed chicks.

rookery
A large group, or colony, of animals breeding in one place. Used sometimes for penguin colonies but also refers to groups of rooks (European birds).

species
A group of animals that share similar characteristics and can breed together to produce fertile young.

streamlined
A smooth, slim shape that cuts through the air or water easily.

subspecies
A species is sometimes divided into even smaller groups called subspecies, which may differ in appearance and live in different areas, although they can still interbreed if they meet.

tobogganing
When a penguin slides on its belly, sometimes pushing itself along with its flippers and feet.

INDEX